WINDSOR
IN OLD PHOTOGRAPHS

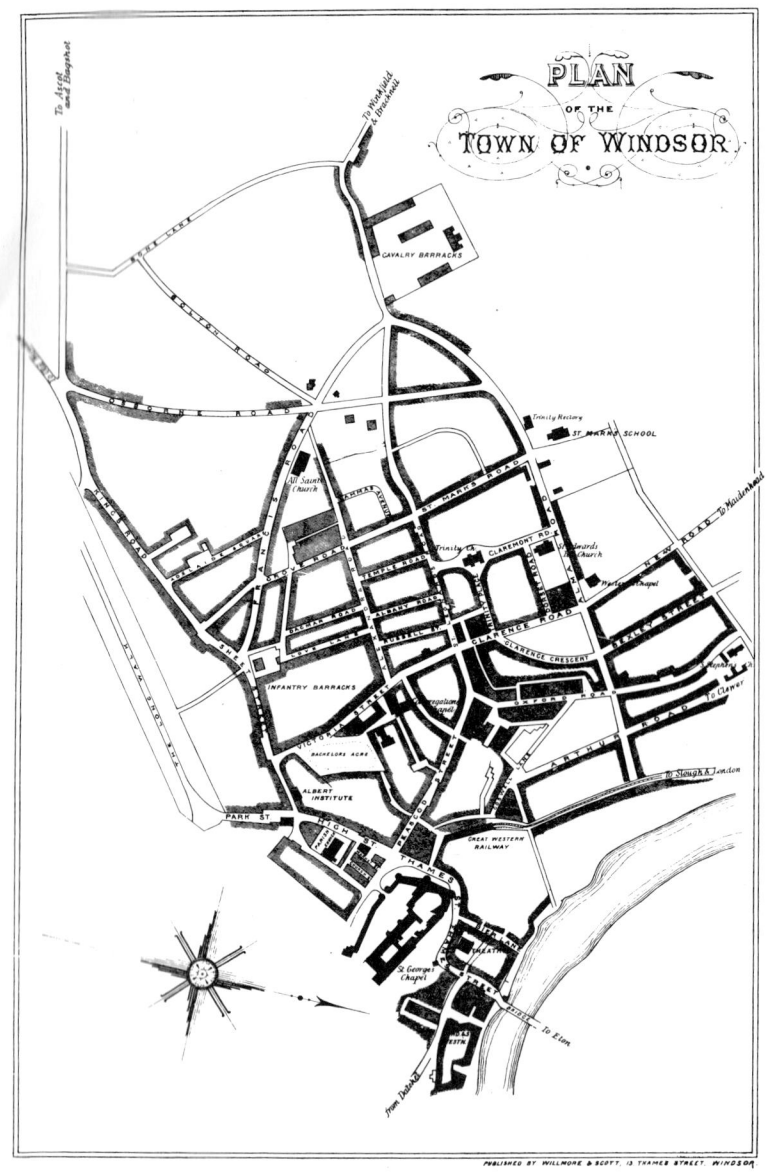

PLAN OF THE TOWN OF WINDSOR

EARLY TWENTIETH-CENTURY WINDSOR

WINDSOR
IN OLD PHOTOGRAPHS

_____COLLECTED BY_____
BERYL HEDGES

ALAN SUTTON
1988

Alan Sutton Publishing Limited
Brunswick Road · Gloucester

First published 1988

British Library Cataloguing in Publication Data

Windsor in old photographs.
1. Berkshire. Windsor, history
I. Hedges, Beryl
942.2'96

ISBN 0-86299-546-9

Typesetting and origination by
Alan Sutton Publishing Limited.
Printed in Great Britain by
WBC Print Limited.

CONTENTS

WINDSOR.

INTRODUCTION

More than five million visitors each year come to Windsor and so the area can surely claim to be one of the most photographed in Britain. Many guide books have been written on Windsor Castle and nearby Eton, and it must be said that most photographs and nearly all of the books feature views of the castle paying little regard to the town of Windsor. In an attempt to rectify this oversight, I have endeavoured in this book to reproduce postcards and photographs depicting the changing face of Windsor, and Windsorians at work and play, over approximately the past 100 years.

Apart from its royal connections, Windsor has for many years had close ties with the British Army, and many are the soldiers who have passed through Combermere and Victoria Barracks both in peace and war, some marrying local girls and setting up home in the town.

The River Thames has always played an important part in the life of the town, mainly as a source of recreation, but on occasion causing havoc and destruction when bursting its banks, as in 1947. For obvious reasons Windsor and Eton are normally bracketed together by most history and guide books, although until recent years the River Thames formed the boundary between Berkshire and Buckinghamshire, with Eton in the latter. Windsor always maintained its own identity, however, until amalgamated with Maidenhead in 1974. Bounded on the north by the river and on the south by the vast expanse of the Great Park, Windsor has developed towards the west from Clewer. I have therefore started this collection with Clewer, as the church is undoubtedly the oldest building in the Royal Borough. Indeed William I leased the land for his fortification in New Windsor which developed into Windsor Castle, from the lord of the manor of Clewer, the rent being paid for generations.

Many books have been written on the Royal Family and the House of Windsor, but it would be impossible not to include here a section on Windsor's royal heritage with so many local and national events involving the people and town of Windsor.

It has been my good fortune over the last twenty years to have associated with many people who share an enthusiasm for the history of the Royal Borough, thereby stimulating my interest and increasing my knowledge. I therefore hope that Windsorians of all ages may find something of enjoyment in these pages and that in some cases the pictures may revive many happy memories.

Old House at the lower end of Peascod Street

SECTION ONE

Clewer

Clewer Church, Windsor
*haplin people say that have sent out twice for that boat
hope that they will get them soon.*

1311 g

WHEN WILLIAM THE CONQUEROR built a ring of castles round London, each one a day's ride from the capital, he chose the chalk cliff in the manor of Clewer for what was to become Windsor Castle. The rent for the land was paid regularly until the sixteenth century. The village of Clewer stretches from the church by the Mill Stream of the River Thames, through Parsonage Lane and Hatch Lane to Clewer Green. The Parish Church of St Andrew (above and below) is the oldest building in the area, probably of Saxon origin and certainly in the Norman style. The ancient font has pea pods carved round it, illustrating that the carver knew that peas were grown locally, a fact which also gives rise to the name of Peascod Street.

St. Andrew's Hospital, Clewer.

THE SITE OF THE HOSPITAL OF ST ANDREW, Clewer, has retained its original conception of care for the sick and elderly, and the new building on the corner of Hatch Lane and Dedworth comprises warden-controlled flats and a day centre.

THE CONVENT OF ST JOHN THE BAPTIST in Hatch Lane, built in the nineteenth century, is little changed. This photograph taken in 1946/7 shows the rural aspect, where a housing estate now stands.

AN INTERIOR VIEW OF ST ANDREW'S HOSPITAL and the cross shows the bed occupied by the writer of the postcard while in the ward. She writes to a friend in 1910 asking for 'something nice'. Some broken china from the hospital, bearing the Cross of St Andrew, can be seen in Clewer Church Museum.

ANOTHER VIEW OF ST ANDREW'S HOSPITAL. This postcard of the same date announces the homecoming of the writer.

CLEWER POLICE STATION stood on the corner of Parsonage Lane and Clarence Road; the boundary wall can still be seen extending along Parsonage Lane. Next to the Bell Inn was Clewer New Town post office, seen here with the postman's bicycle outside. The village had its own postmark, seen here c. 1910.

THE CHURCH OF CLEWER ST STEPHEN was consecrated in 1874, the parish having been formed in 1872. The architect, Henry Woodyer, also built the chapel in the Convent of St John in Hatch Lane. The church and the sisters of the convent always worked closely together to help the poor in this area of the town.

CLEWER COURT was this imposing house on a prime site by the River Thames. Occupied in the 1960s by the RikkiTik Club, it has now been replaced by the Leisure Pool.

THE DINING HALL OF ST ANDREW'S HOSPITAL, though simple, shows the hand of a kindly Matron with pictures on the walls and aspidistras on the tables.

THE WORK IN THE PARISH OF ST STEPHEN led eventually to the founding of St Stephen's High School in 1882 by Sister Miriam and Miss du Pre. The building (shown above and below) was opened in 1889 for 100 day girls and 50 boarders, who were known as 'Robins' because of their brown and red uniforms. The school closed in 1934.

SECTION TWO

The Town

THE MEDIEVAL PATTERN OF THE COBBLED STREETS at the gates of the castle still exists though Priest Street is now St Alban's Street and Fish Street is now Church Street, seen here. Although there may be modern shop fronts, many old buildings exist behind the façades.

THE PRESENT PARISH CHURCH OF ST JOHN THE BAPTIST replaced a very much older one in 1822. An innovation at the time was the use of cast iron for the interior columns that support the galleries. The present chancel was added fifty years later by Teulon. Since this photograph was taken a war memorial to the fallen of both world wars has been erected in the churchyard behind the carriages.

THE GUILDHALL (on this and the opposite page) was designed in 1687 by Sir Thomas Fitch, and on his death was completed by Sir Christopher Wren, who had spent his boyhood in Windsor when his father was Dean of St George's Chapel. All civic affairs were carried out here until the Royal Borough was amalgamated with Maidenhead in 1974, forming the Royal Borough of Windsor and Maidenhead. The Court of Quarter Session was held in the Guildhall Chamber until 1971. Portraits of sovereigns and their consorts line the walls of the chamber, the latest being a fine likeness of Prince Philip, added in 1988. The Corn Exchange was opened and the windows removed in 1951. The latest major 'spring clean' began in 1982 when the museum was closed, its contents moved to a store in Tinker's Lane, Dedworth, and the room itself transformed into a conference room.

Windsor Guildhall

Mayor's Parlour

THE FLOWER SELLER, all that is left of the Windsor street market in the Guildhall area, sells her wares on the other side of the Guildhall in front of Market House. The postman stops for a chat and a man looks out from the dormer window.

Windsor, High Street.

A S
WDR 22

IT IS NOW THE 1950s. Cars are parked in High Street and travellers wait for buses outside the parish church. However, there is still a cyclist on the road, albeit a more modern model.

QUEEN ANNE'S STATUE can be seen in a niche on the Guildhall and the Corn Exchange still has windows.

THE SITE ON CASTLE HILL OF THE OLD MARKET CROSS, now marked by the statue of Queen Victoria, has always been the central place where proclamations and announcements are made, and a meeting place for all.

AT THE FOOT OF CURFEW TOWER a keen eye will find a cross carved in the stone, in remembrance of a young Windsor butcher, Mark Fytton, who was hanged from the tower in the reign of Henry VIII.

Curfew Tower,   Windsor Castle.

THAMES STREET still retains the iron hoops in the kerbside to prevent the carriages of the horse-drawn taxis slipping down the hill.

Entrance to Hundred Steps, Windsor.

IN THAMES STREET at the turn of the century the horses were provided with a trough for a drink before hauling their load up the hill. The gateway to the Hundred Steps is now closed to the public.

HORSE BRAKES, GROWLERS AND FLYS OF ALL DESCRIPTIONS drawn up at the foot of Castle Hill during Ascot Week. The horse bus with a Liverpool Street sign was down from London for the races.

THE CASTLE HILL. — WINDSOR.
AND JUBILEE STATUE OF THE QUEEN.

A PICTURE ALBUM gives a delightful insight into the evening promenade at the turn of the century. It looks as if there is a crocodile of young ladies coming down the hill. Marshall's shop is on the site of that of Charles Knight senior, bookseller friend of George III, whose son, also Charles Knight, later founded the *Windsor & Eton Express*.

Thames Street, Windsor

THE CROWN is the public house on the right. The licence of this pub was surrendered and transferred to The Windsor Lad in Maidenhead Road when it opened.

THE PLAYHOUSE THEATRE was one of three cinemas in Windsor. All have now been redeveloped, this one being the last to be demolished.

TWO PHOTOGRAPHS PRIOR TO SEPARATE REDEVELOPMENT IN WINDSOR. Above: River Street when houses had been pulled down and before the car park was laid out. Below: Goswell Road before King Edward Court was built. As there are fewer and shorter trains now, some of the disused tracks have become a car park and the huge domed roof of the station contains Madame Tussaud's Royalty and Empire Exhibition.

THE RIVER STREET AND GOSWELLS AREA near the River Thames was densely populated, but the houses in River Street were demolished and replaced by a car park in the 1920s. The inhabitants were rehoused in new properties in Dedworth. St Saviours Church was a mission church of Holy Trinity, and there was also a small school for a short time, St Mary's.

THE QUIET SCENE OF THE GOSWELLS was later laid out by the council as tennis courts and a bowling green. Some of the land is the property of the National Trust, which protects the uninterrupted view of the castle from the river.

Castle Hill, Windsor

TWO POLICEMEN have time to stop for a chat early in the century. Windsor was one of the first towns to have gas lamps.

THE NEW INN HOTEL was reputed to have been one of the oldest in the town and was situated at the end of Park Street. The building was pulled down in 1931.

CASTLE HILL early this century was a popular place for visitors and townsfolk alike. A school party can be seen in the lower left of the picture.

THE WINDSOR POLICE AND FIRE STATIONS and appropriately named 'The Old Court' now house the Windsor Arts Centre. The fire station is now in St Mark's Road and the police station and magistrates court are in Alma Road.

A CAB RANK stood outside the parish church with a shelter for the drivers. The County Bank later became the Westminster Bank.

W. J. DANIEL & CO. LTD. are still in Peascod Street today. Daniel's sales were and still are eagerly awaited by local families.

PEASCOD STREET. This card with a 1906 postmark shows the popular shops of Walker's the grocer and Wm. Creak. There is a road sweeper in the foreground.

Windsor Borough Police Force. March. 1930.

WINDSOR BOROUGH POLICE FORCE 1930.

MR A.W. BULL AND MR H. BURGESS stand in the doorway of Wells Stores in Kings Road.

WINDSOR BRIDGE was closed in 1970, being unsafe for vehicular traffic, and the area was pedestrianized. Wren's Old House Hotel now extends to the promenade to the right of the picture.

Riverside Gardens, Windsor.

BELOW THE BRIDGE on the Windsor side before the promenade was made up. Behind the trees on the right of the picture was the brewery.

THE STAR AND GARTER has now been demolished and replaced by shops. In its heyday it was a famous training headquarters for such boxers as Len Harvey, Jack Doyle and latterly Sugar Ray Robinson. Mr Harry Drake, a Windsorian, was a sparring partner to many famous boxers including Jack Dempsey.

Trade and Industry

ENTERPRISING MOTOR ENGINEERS set up garages and workshops on the outskirts of the town as Windsor developed. Martin's Garage was in St Leonard's Road where Lammas Court is now.

BARKER'S GARAGE, on the corner of William Street and Victoria Street, was pulled down to make way for Blazer's nightclub and a modern petrol station.

CALEY'S SHOP in the High Street sold a different range in 1900, and this picture of the furniture showroom displays a chair for sale at 7s. 6d.

THE NORTH SIDE OF SHEET STREET was rebuilt in Victorian times when the Royal Albert Institute was opened in 1880 as a memorial to Queen Victoria's consort.

Windsor, Peascod Street and Castle

A VIEW LOOKING ALONG PEASCOD STREET to the castle, eighty years ago.

THE LADIES MANTLE DEPARTMENT of Caleys.

CALEYS FUNERAL SERVICE. These two pictures were taken at the beginning of the century. Caleys is now part of the John Lewis Partnership.

WINDSOR FIRE BRIGADE, in common with most brigades in the country, was a volunteer force and was merged into the NFS in 1939. This is the Windsor brigade's stand at the Royal Agricultural Show in the Home Park, June 1913.

MAXWELL'S STORE was in Alexandra Road.

MR JOHN MAXWELL, another enterprising Windsor engineer, opened a garage in Clarence Road, near the corner of Parsonage Lane.

A GROUP OF POSTMEN, POSTBOYS AND A POSTMISTRESS, outside the post office in High Street in 1897. This office closed in 1966.

A VIEW OF OXFORD ROAD which, with other streets, was demolished to make way for Ward Royal.

MR EDWARD CUNNINGHAM stands behind the counter of Lawrence's, his friend's tobacco shop, in Oxford Road.

WINDSOR SORTING OFFICE in 1955. The new post office in Peascod Street, opened in 1966 by the Mayor, is on part of the site of Wm. Creak's shop.

THE ADVERTISEMENT PROUDLY ANNOUNCES that the White Hart Hotel could cater for any occasion.

LAYTON'S TEA ROOMS AND RESTAURANT on the corner of Station Approach and Thames Street was a popular venue. Behind the tea rooms, adjoining the station, was a long bar known as the Rat Trap.

WELLS STORES also housed King's Road Post Office. Messrs. Hardwick, A.W. Bull and H. Burgess stand in the doorway. The brake mechanism of the trade bicycle was controlled by back-pedalling.

THE WINDOW OF THE SHOP IS NOW DRESSED FOR CHRISTMAS and Mr Bull is joined by A. Wells, W.J. Wells and W.P. Tracy. Braddle's bakery was a favourite in the early 1900s.

THIS GROUP OF BUILDERS pose for a photograph outside the property they are working on in Dedworth after the First World War.

WILLIAM CREAK'S ESTABLISHMENT in Peascod Street was on the site of the old Pilgrim Place.
Opposite was the pathway known as 'Creak's Passage'.

ADVERTISEMENTS showing services offered by shops and businesses early this century.

TWO LOCAL DUSTMEN with their cart. The depot was in Love Lane, then moved to Alma Road and is now in Tinkers Lane, Dedworth.

A GROUP OF MEN gather in Peascod Street in the 1930s. They were able to buy postcards from a shop there and resell them in Thames Street from the kerbside. Later some of the men found employment building Imperial Road, which runs from Winkfield Road to Clarence Road.

A WINDSOR DEPARTMENT STORE proudly displays the Royal Warrant.

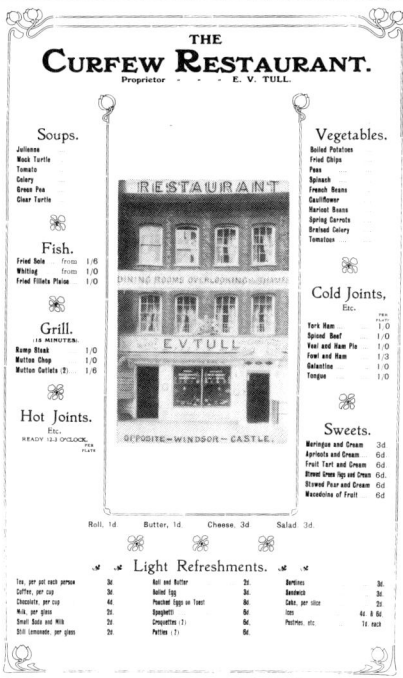

TULL'S ESTABLISHMENT IN THAMES STREET also sold delicious home-made chocolates; at Christmas and Easter among other occasions Mr Tull made chocolate pictures, animals and birds as a display.

WELLMAN'S STORES was on the corner of Peascod Street and William Street.

Windsor, Thames Street, Riverholme Hotel Annexe

RIVERHOLME HOTEL is now part of Wren's Old House Hotel.

THIS SCENE AT THE SOUTHERN RAILWAY STATION has altered little except that the horse-drawn taxi cabs and the delivery cart would be motorised today. The large coalyard beside the station is now a car park.

MESSRS. H. WAY & SONS, goldsmiths and silversmiths, established their business in Thames Street in 1769, and proudly announced in their advertisements in the years before the First World War that they held the most complete stock in the neighbourhood.

NOS. 37 AND 39 SHEET STREET were occupied by Surplice's Garage. Mr John Maxwell, third from the left, later opened his own business in Clarence Road.

SECTION FOUR
Leisure

A CARNIVAL AND FÊTE was held in Alexandra Gardens in 1988, reviving the days shown in this picture, when the band played in the bandstand and the sun always shone.

Windsor Castle and Alexandra Gardens

THIS VIEW OF ALEXANDRA GARDENS from Barry Avenue and the railway arches has a postmark of 1920, when the promenade had been laid out. The writer was enjoying a quick tour of Windsor and then heading on to Henley.

THE REVD C. HAMILTON, vicar of Windsor 1921–40, presides over Windsor Parish Church Bazaar in the garden of Abbey House, Sheet Street.

THE RIVERSIDE GARDENS were very popular for relaxation and not as crowded as today! One family cycled regularly from Chertsey to Windsor, which was quite a distance.

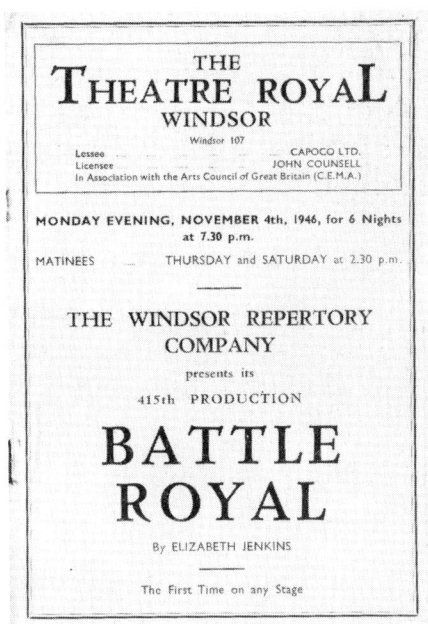

THE
THEATRE ROYAL
WINDSOR
Windsor 107

Lessee .... CAPOCO LTD.
Licensee .... JOHN COUNSELL
In Association with the Arts Council of Great Britain (C.E.M.A.)

**MONDAY EVENING, NOVEMBER 4th, 1946, for 6 Nights
at 7.30 p.m.**

MATINEES ..... THURSDAY and SATURDAY at 2.30 p.m.

THE WINDSOR REPERTORY
COMPANY
presents its
415th PRODUCTION

BATTLE
ROYAL

By ELIZABETH JENKINS

The First Time on any Stage

PROGRAMME - - PRICE THREEPENCE

THE THEATRE ROYAL, Windsor, (here and on opposite page) has always provided good entertainment and many Windsorians have regular seats for each production. The management always supported the Windsor & Eton Operatic Society, who performed *The Mikado* (below) in 1926 and *The Gondoliers* in 1935.

THE PIRATES OF PENZANCE. JANY 1912. J.B.V

MANY TYPES OF ENTERTAINMENT were also provided at the Royal Albert Institute in Sheet Street. There was a ballroom and rooms for smaller gatherings, and local amateur dramatic and operatic societies presented their productions there. Before being demolished the rooms in the Institute were used for educational purposes by the then East Berks College.

THE WINDSOR

OPERATIC DRAMATIC

SOCIETY

ROYAL ALBERT INSTITUTE

Patrons :

HER ROYAL HIGHNESS PRINCESS ALICE COUNTESS OF ATHLONE.
HER HIGHNESS PRINCESS HELENA VICTORIA
HER HIGHNESS PRINCESS MARIE LOUISE
BRIG.-GEN. THE EARL OF ATHLONE, K.G., G.C.B., G.C.V.O., G.C.M.G., D.S.O., A.D.C.

President : MAJOR J. B. S. BOURNE MAY.

Vice-Presidents :

THE VERY REV. THE DEAN OF WINDSOR.	R. J. W. HARTLEY, Esq.
J. CAVE, Esq.	HENRY G. LEY, Esq., M.A., MUS.DOC.
W. B. CHAPLIN, Esq.	W. E. MASON, Esq.
A. H. S. COWLEY, Esq.	T. MUNDY, Esq.
Miss L. COWLEY.	F. A. OGILVY, Esq., F.R.C.O.
The Rev. CANON A. C. DEANE, M.A., F.R.S.I.	S. F. OXLEY, Esq.
E. C. DURANT, Esq., M.V.O., J.P.	A. A. SOMERVILLE, Esq., M.P.
W. H. HARRIS, Esq., M.A., MUS. DOC.	Mrs. E. B. STIMSON.
Rev. C. H. HAMILTON, M.A.	A. L. WIGAN, Esq.

"Love and Learning"

An Operette

Written and Composed by Mr. R. STILL, M.A., Mus. Bac.

THURSDAY, FRIDAY AND SATURDAY

MAY 11th, 12th and 13th, 1939

PROGRAMME

THE FERRYMAN plies across to the Brocas at Eton and the owner of the punts waits for customers.

Thames Side, Windsor.

THE TICKET OFFICE FOR SALTER'S STEAMERS is on the right of the picture and the boats wait in the water by the boards which display their destinations. In the distance, along the roadway, is a public house now known as the Donkey House. The entrance to the railway goods yard and coal depot can be seen beyond.

EPISODE 2. ROSA PRESENTS ROSES TO QUEEN ELEANOR.

EPISODE TWO OF A PRODUCTION BY LOCAL SCHOOLCHILDREN in the grounds of Long Walk House, to celebrate the coronation of King George V in 1911. Mr R. Bull is fourth from the left.

DAY OUTINGS from public houses were very popular and in this undated photograph the passengers are ready to board their coach outside The Herts Arms, which was in St Leonard's Road by Spinner's Walk. They were off to Goodwood for the races.

MRS PARKER AND HER NEIGHBOURS worked for this street party in Dedworth to celebrate the coronation of King George VI and Queen Elizabeth in 1936.

EMPIRE DAY IN THE HOME PARK, pre-1914, when all the Windsor schools gathered to celebrate. The photographer has left a camera on the grass.

IN ANOTHER PART OF WINDSOR GREAT PARK a party of Brownies from St Edward's pack enjoy a picnic during the 1930s.

DOG SHOWS, PONY AND HORSE SHOWS AND THE ROSE SHOW have long been held in the Great Park. Later polo and other equestrian events were organised on Smiths Lawn.

Aug 1907

THE WINDSOR FIRE BRIGADE SPORTS held in Victoria Barracks in Victoria Street, August 1907.

ANOTHER PICTURE OF SPORTS HELD IN THE BARRACKS.

THE POND HAS DISAPPEARED FROM ALEXANDRA GARDENS as have the cannon and railings which were removed in the last war.

Churches and Schools

ST STEPHEN'S HIGH SCHOOL was in Vansittart Road. Its laboratory seems very well equipped.

THE NAME OF ST ANNE'S SCHOOL, which had been etched in the stone over the doorway in Clewer Fields, had nearly worn away when this photograph was taken – shortly before the school, by then known as Holy Trinity School, was pulled down.

A HAPPY GROUP OF CHILDREN AND THEIR SUNDAY SCHOOL TEACHERS outside the Old Tin Chapel in Dedworth. Lit by gas and with a single gas-ring to boil water on, it had a large congregation, who now worship in a new chapel in Smiths Lane.

A. L. C. Wintle.   E. Bazalgette.   I. C. Findlay.   G. M. Mayne.   K. F. Bishop.   F. St. A. Hartley.
C. W. C. Hickie.   P. B. Bass.   E. S. H. Morris.   T. A. T. Biggood.   G. L. Findlay.

IMPERIAL SERVICE COLLEGE FIRST XI in 1913. The college occupied Kipling Building, a chapel and boarding houses in Alma Road. The council later used Kipling Building as offices and in 1974 the land was sold. Windsor Police Station and Magistrates Court are on part of the site.

WINDSOR BOYS SCHOOL moved from these buildings near Holy Trinity Church to the present school in Maidenhead Road in 1939.

WINDSOR BOYS SCHOOL undefeated hockey team 1957, 2nd XI.

WINDSOR BOYS SCHOOL. Opening of the new buildings in 1939.

THE INTERIOR OF WINDSOR PARISH CHURCH shows the cast-iron columns that Charles Hollis used in 1822 when the church was rebuilt.

St. JOHN'S PARISH CHURCH

WINDSOR.

Rev. J. H. ELLISON, M.A.

THE REVD J.H. ELLISON was a well-loved vicar of Windsor from 1855 to 1876, and his curate, S.J. Stone, wrote many hymns while in the town. The best loved, one of a series, is called 'The Church's One Foundation'.

A PARTY OF SCHOOLCHILDREN AT QUEEN ANNE'S GATE watch a re-enactment by postmen in Edwardian dress to celebrate the Golden Jubilee of British Air Mail on 9 September 1961.

where I was christened

HOLY TRINITY CHURCH in Trinity Place, consecrated in 1842, was built to serve the growing town and also the army garrisoned at Combermere and Victoria Barracks.

TO ACCOMMODATE THE LARGE CONGREGATION it was necessary to include galleries in the design of Holy Trinity and the church can seat over 1000 people. Today many banners and memorials to soldiers who have fallen in wars since the Crimea can be seen in the church.

THE REVD JOHN STOUGHTON, minister of the Congregational Church in William Street, wrote a history of Windsor in 1844. He was a great friend of W. Redford Harris who founded Clewer House, a school for young gentlemen, in St Leonard's Road. The cedar tree outside a house opposite Lammas Court is all that remains of this establishment.

THE CONGREGATIONAL CHAPEL. This photograph was taken shortly before its demolition in the 1970s. The lineal descendant of the Congregational Church, the United Reformed Church, has a chapel in the new complex since built on the site.

ELMFIELD was demolished when King's Road roundabout was laid out in 1966–7. Built for Henry Darvill, a solicitor and town clerk, it had a worn date-stone of 1863 or 1865. It was bought for Windsor Girls Grammar School in 1919 or 1920 and is seen here in 1960.

CARFAX (photographed in 1960) was an older building than Elmfield and was acquired for the Girls Grammar School after World War II. The Gables was bought in 1959 and the school continued in these buildings and St Martin's until the first two forms moved to the new school in Imperial Road in 1964. The whole school had moved by 1965.

A GROUP OF WINDSOR HIGH SCHOOL GIRLS with Miss K. Shawcross photographed in 1950.

ST AGNES CHURCH, Spital, in 1907.

All Saints' Church, Windsor

ALL SAINT'S CHURCH, Frances Road, was designed by Arthur Bromfield, possibly with the help of Thomas Hardy. It was built because the parish church seating capacity of 1600 was not sufficient, and Canon Ellison planned a new church. Queen Victoria made a handsome contribution and her eldest daughter, the Empress Frederick of Prussia, laid the foundation stone in 1863.

THE ROYAL FREE SENIOR SCHOOL left this building in Bachelor's Acre in 1967. The girls had left in 1930 for either Clewer St Stephen or Princess Margaret Rose School in Vansittart Road and the building was finally vacated by the Junior School in 1987.

A VISIT TO PRINCESS MARGARET ROSE SCHOOL by Her Royal Highness, Princess Margaret, on 13 July 1956. Miss Hilda Jones, the headmistress, is followed by Canon Creed Meredith and the Mayor.

A SCHOOL TRIP FOR ROYAL FREE BOYS in 1954.

A ROYAL VISIT TO PRINCESS MARGARET ROSE SCHOOL on 11 July 1944.

SECTION SIX

Flood and Fire

THE FLOODS: THE VALLEY OF THE THAMES FROM THE ROUND TOWER, WINDSOR CASTLE

THE HEAVY RAINS OF SOME WINTERS have resulted in terrible floods. This picture from Windsor Castle shows the broken river banks in 1873.

DUKWs were used in 1947 to rescue families in Oxford Road and Alma Road.

THE RUINS OF THE FIRE AT WINDSOR ON SUNDAY, APRIL 28, 1907. *Downer Photo*

FIRE WAS ANOTHER DREADFUL HAZARD. These pictures show the Volunteer Fire Brigade fighting the fire, and the remains when it had been controlled.

THE FIRE AT WINDSOR ON SUNDAY APRIL 28TH 1907. *Downer, Copyright Photo.*

EATRE ROYAL, WINDSOR, BURNT FEB. 15TH 1908.

THE THEATRE ROYAL suffered the same fate in 1908, but happily was rebuilt.

THE FLOODS in 1947, a view from the railway.

POSTAL DELIVERY.

A SKETCH OF THE POSTAL DELIVERY during floods in 1875.

DELIVERING COALS AT THE WINDOWS.

THE LATE FLOODS AT WINDSOR.

AS THE WATER BEGAN TO RECEDE, the coal-man resumed his delivery! Punts were used in 1875 as public transport.

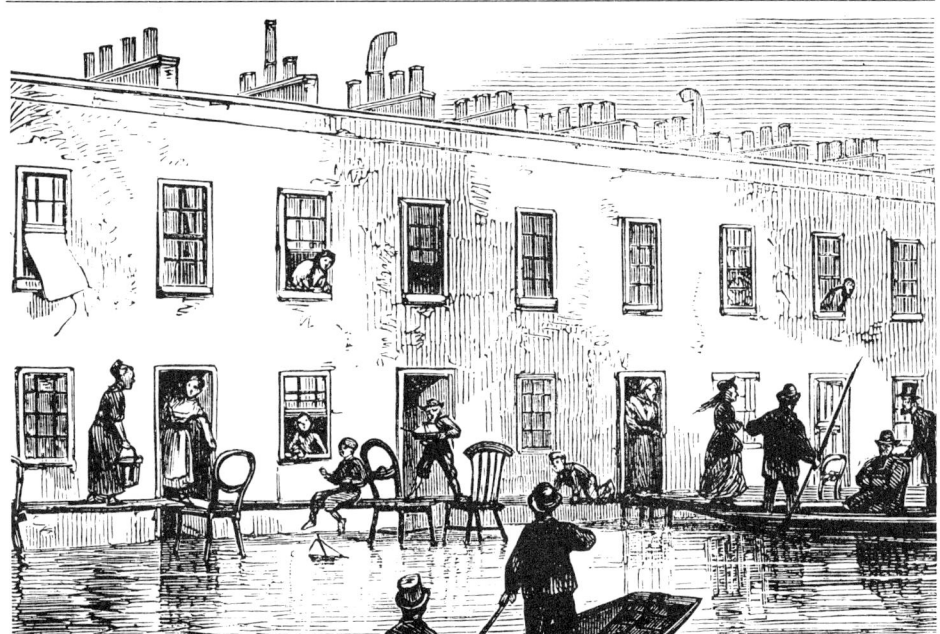

EVER RESOURCEFUL, the residents made bridges of planks and chairs. The lady with a pail gingerly walks the plank, while the young man quietly smokes his clay pipe and waits patiently for the punt.

Local and National Events

PRIZE-GIVING ON SPORTS DAY 1909 at Windsor County Boys School. The Senior Challenge Cup was won by K. Cartland who also won the long distance race of nine and one-fifth miles. Mrs G.H. Peters, wife of the chairman of the Governors, presented the prizes. The headmaster was G.H. Wade, MA.

KING EDWARD VII had laid the foundation stone of the hospital in 1908, and by 1909 the children's ward, chapel and operating theatre were open. This hospital replaced the old infirmary in Victoria Street adjoining the Dispensary.

A BED WAS ENDOWED in King Edward VII Hospital to commemorate the first UK Aerial Post in 1911.

MR HAMEL GETTING READY TO START. Nº 2. JRTS.

1911

ON 9 SEPTEMBER 1911 three aeroplanes left Hendon for Windsor with the first aerial post in the United Kingdom. Gustav Hamel was the chief pilot, the second plane was piloted by Driver and the third crashed. Windsor postmen were waiting in the Park to collect the mail from Hamel.

Sept 1911   MR. DRIVER, ARRIVES   12

Sept 1911   MR. CRESWELL, AND HIS BIPLANE.   No.1. J.R.75.

THE START OF THE MARATHON RACE from Windsor to London on 14 July 1908 in the grounds of Windsor Castle. The distance was 26 miles.

THE MARATHON LEAVES THE CASTLE on its way to London. Dorando, No 19, was disqualified and Hayes was declared the winner. The policeman standing near Queen Victoria's statue wears a straw helmet. They were worn in summer by Windsor police and some other police forces.

MR GUSTAV HAMEL and his aeroplane.

THE MAYOR, ALDERMEN AND COUNCILLORS leave the parish church after a civic service in 1906.

The Army in Windsor

THE ARMY has always had very close ties with the town of Windsor, the Duke of Edinburgh's Royal regiment and the Brigade of Guards having received the Freedom of the Borough in the 1960s. In the picture the streets are decorated to welcome the soldiers home from the Second World War, and the band led them through the town.

MANY WINDSOR MEN SERVED IN THE ROYAL BERKSHIRE REGIMENT in both world wars, and this photograph shows the men training at Beaulieu in 1907.

A SILENT CROWD LINE THE STREETS for a military funeral. The procession from Holy Trinity was moving to watch, with the unsaddled charger following his master's coffin.

THE BAND OF THE IRISH GUARDS march along Victoria Street led by their mascot. The rounded building they are passing was the Dispensary and Infirmary.

THE BAND OF THE 2ND LIFE GUARDS lead the soldiers to Church Parade from Combermere Barracks in St Leonard's Road to Holy Trinity Church.

COMBERMERE BARRACKS were built in the early nineteenth century, the Blues being the first occupants in 1804. By 1870 they had been reconstructed and enlarged and were formally named 'Combermere' Barracks in 1900. To facilitate the moving of the cavalry from Windsor to London, fourteen doors were specially made in the Southern Railway station when it was built in 1851.

THE 2ND LIFE GUARDS parade past the police station on 15 August 1914 on their way through the town to fight in the First World War.

THE 2ND LIFE GUARDS march out of Combermere Barracks. The soldier on the extreme right is Stancombe Rawlings.

THE INFANTRY BARRACKS were also built in the early nineteenth century, with many additions up to the First World War. The barracks were named Victoria Barracks in 1889. They have now been demolished.

ALTHOUGH IT WAS A VERY WET DAY, the people of Windsor stood to hear the military band on Castle Hill. At Christmas, the carol singing on Castle Hill is always accompanied by a military band.

BEFORE THE WAR, in 1913, the Household Cavalry were reviewed by King George V in the Great Park.

HRH THE DUKE OF CONNAUGHT inspecting the heavy guns in the Great Park in 1907.

A PARADE OF EX-SERVICEMEN, in about 1912, after a church service. The little boy in a dark coat being held by his father is Mr R. Bull.

THE FRIENDLY RIVALRY between the men of the town and army was shown in the football matches. Here is one between Windsor & Eton FC and the Grenadier Guards.

NERAL OF TRUMPET MAJ. S.J. GOODALL   2ND LIFE GUARDS WINDSOR
FEB. 12

ANOTHER IMPRESSIVE MILITARY FUNERAL took place, that of Major S.J. Goodall, 2nd Life Guards, on 12 February 1912.

DECORATIONS OUTSIDE THE THEATRE ROYAL in Thames Street to welcome home the soldiers after the war.

Combermere Barracks, Windsor, Officers' Quarters

COMBERMERE BARRACKS. The writer of this postcard, in 1911, says 'Our barracks a fine place in summer but very dull in winter.'

Royalty in Windsor

THE VISIT OF KING GEORGE V AND QUEEN MARY to Windsor after their coronation in 1911. The young Princess Mary stands next to the Queen with one of her brothers next to her. They are greeted at Queen Victoria's statue by the Mayor, Aldermen and Councillors. Note the cobbled street.

AWAITING ANOTHER STATE OCCASION is the Mayor of the Royal Borough of Windsor, Sir Frederick Dyson. On the right, Stanley Oxley talks to Lady Dyson.

OR CARS IN LONG WALK FOR ROYAL GARDEN PARTY WINDSOR. 1908

WINDSOR CASTLE was the venue for many royal garden parties, and on these occasions the Long Walk had to be used to park the visitors' cars.

KING GEORGE V AND QUEEN MARY drive past Layton's Restaurant into Station Approach after a visit to Windsor Castle.

A LARGE GATHERING of townspeople, soldiers and civic dignitaries hear the proclamation of King George V beneath the statue of Queen Victoria. All public announcements and proclamations are made on this site of the Old Market Cross.

A PRE-1914 PARADE OF BOY SCOUTS in the Park. Scouts still gather annually for a service in St George's Chapel, Windsor Castle.

THE FUNERAL PROCESSION OF THE LATE KING EDWARD VII.
HIGH STREET, WINDSOR.

THE LONG FUNERAL PROCESSION OF KING EDWARD VII. The gun carriage carrying the coffin was pulled by sailors, as at the funeral of Queen Victoria. The King was buried in St George's Chapel.

FUNERAL OF THE LATE KING EDWARD VII AT WINDSOR
COPYRIGHT.

PRINCE HENRY, High Steward of the Royal Borough, accompanies his mother, Queen Mary, on a drive through Windsor, on the occasion of thanksgiving for the recovery of King George V from severe illness.

SECTION TEN

Around Windsor

THE COCKPIT RESTAURANT in Eton High Street is a very old, and well-maintained, building. The old post box is still outside. The town of Eton is far older than the college which was founded by Henry VI in 1440.

THE BAND AT ETON FIRE BRIGADE SPORTS prepares for a concert early this century.

ETON WICK stretches from Eton to Boveney and, at the time of this photograph, small shops were being opened along the long road. The animals from the farms crossed the road to graze in the fields and, at harvest time, the children were happy to escape from school and help, as in many other schools throughout the land.

A VERY FAMILIAR LANDMARK to boatmen and townsfolk of Windsor & Eton was the Bridge House Hotel, adjoining the bridge and boathouses on the Eton side of the River Thames.

Proprietor, **GILBERT RUSSELL, Eton, Windsor.**

THE BRIDGE HOUSE HOTEL. This advertisement maintained that it was the only First Class Hotel in Eton and very conveniently placed.

SURLY HALL was a very well-patronised hotel on the river between Clewer and Boveney, much loved by the boys of Eton College who arrived by boat. The road from Clewer to Maidenhead was known as Surly Hall Road.

MONKEY ISLAND HOTEL AT BRAY was another favourite hotel on the River Thames which is still popular with visitors by water and road.

THE BELLS OF OUSLEY HOTEL stands on the road through Old Windsor to Runnymede, though sadly the river frontage is no longer as pictured here. The hotel was hit by a flying bomb in 1944 and much rebuilding was required.

AT THE COMING OF THE RAILWAYS to Windsor the old Datchet Bridge was demolished and two new ones built: the Victoria Bridge, from Windsor into Datchet via Datchet Road, and Albert Bridge, from Datchet into Old Windsor.

THE TAPESTRIES were built in the 1880s to house the Royal Windsor Tapestry Manufactory. Weavers were brought from France for this venture, and they were housed in the cottages, the main weaving hall being in the centre. Prince Leopold was a great supporter of the scheme as were other members of the Royal Family. Sadly, after about ten years and with the death of its patron, Prince Leopold, the Tapestries closed down, and now the hall has been made into flats.

QUEEN ALEXANDRA arriving for a visit to Old Windsor hospital. The nurses line up on the grass and the band is ready to play the National Anthem. A few local people stand by the gate. The hospital is a long walk from the village.

ST. LUKE'S ROAD, OLD WINDSOR.

FROM STRAIGHT ROAD, St Luke's Road winds towards Crimp Hill and the school and hospital. The post office is little changed today.

THE ROYAL ASCOT HOTEL was opened in 1863 and stood on the main road from Ascot to Bracknell. It was extremely busy when there was a race meeting at Ascot, especially so when the Royal Family attended the June races. There was stabling in the yard and, although the hotel has been demolished, it is said that a horse can be heard neighing occasionally!

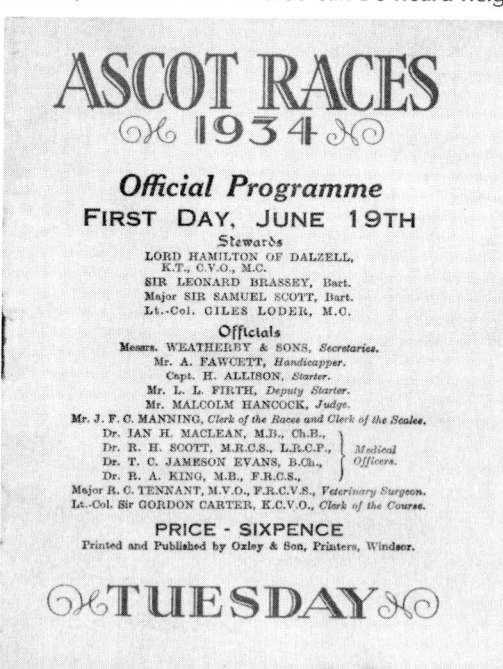

ASCOT RACES
❧ 1934 ❧

Official Programme
FIRST DAY, JUNE 19TH
Stewards
LORD HAMILTON OF DALZELL,
K.T., C.V.O., M.C.
SIR LEONARD BRASSEY, Bart.
Major SIR SAMUEL SCOTT, Bart.
Lt.-Col. GILES LODER, M.C.

Officials
Messrs. WEATHERBY & SONS, *Secretaries.*
Mr. A. FAWCETT, *Handicapper.*
Capt. H. ALLISON, *Starter.*
Mr. L. L. FIRTH, *Deputy Starter.*
Mr. MALCOLM HANCOCK, *Judge.*
Mr. J. F. C. MANNING, *Clerk of the Races and Clerk of the Scales.*
Dr. IAN H. MACLEAN, M.B., Ch.B.,
Dr. R. H. SCOTT, M.R.C.S., L.R.C.P., *Medical*
Dr. T. C. JAMESON EVANS, B.Ch., *Officers.*
Dr. R. A. KING, M.B., F.R.C.S.,
Major R. C. TENNANT, M.V.O., F.R.C.V.S., *Veterinary Surgeon.*
Lt.-Col. Sir GORDON CARTER, K.C.V.O., *Clerk of the Course.*

PRICE - SIXPENCE
Printed and Published by Oxley & Son, Printers, Windsor.

❧ TUESDAY ❧

THE ROYAL ENCLOSURE AND GRAND STAND, ASCOT, 1897

THE ROYAL BOX AND GRANDSTAND have been rebuilt since this photograph was taken of a meeting in 1897, with people crowding the enclosures.

Ascot Races.

THE TENTS ON ASCOT HEATH with racegoers lining the course each side in 1907. Another stand had been built, later to be replaced by the present one.

No. *197* *Railway no 1*
Clever without

WINDSOR & ASCOT RAILWAY.

SIR,

I BEG to acknowledge the receipt, on or before the 15th of December 1897, of your application to me in reference to the above-mentioned proposed undertaking, and I request you will return me to Parliament as

* *Dissenting* _____ in reference thereto.

Your obedient Servant,

Mrs E Lewis

_____

* Here insert the word "assenting," "dissenting," or "neuter," as the case may require.

THE WINDSOR & ASCOT RAILWAY PROJECT never materialised although it cropped up on a number of occasions. There were already two stations in Windsor and no room for another, and, although it would bring people to the town, it would leave the cabbies without fares on race days. So the arguments went on and the railway was not built.

St Leonards.

the Seat of William Dawson Esq.

THE ST LEONARD'S ESTATE was later owned by the Dodge family. Billy Smart developed it into what the present owners have named Royal Windsor Safari Park. This provides a very interesting and popular day out for visitors from home and abroad.

WINDSOR CASTLE FROM LONG WALK.   H.3995.

THE LONG WALK after the elms had been cut down in 1940 due to disease. Later an avenue of plane and horse chestnuts was planted as replacement.

Long Walk, Windsor.

A SCENE IN THE LONG WALK near the Park Street entrance in Edwardian times.

CUMBERLAND LODGE, one of the many large houses in Windsor Great Park, was the home of Prince and Princess Christian. Many alterations have been made and it is now a conference centre.

THE LODGE at the Bishopsgate entrance to Windsor Great Park is very much the same today. Special fences have been erected within the Park to the left of this picture, as the deer which were taken away during the Second World War were reintroduced in 1979.

THE GATEKEEPER stands by his lodge at Blacknest Gate, the entrance to the Park from Ascot. Through the gates is Virginia Water, laid out under the direction of the Duke of Cumberland in the eighteenth century.

THE DEER WANDERED FREELY IN THE PARK before being taken away during the Second World War. They were returned in 1979 in enclosed land.

THE LONG WALK, WINDSOR.

THE LONG WALK. The pond in the foreground has now been filled in.

WINDSOR CASTLE FROM ROMNEY LOCK

A VIEW OF WINDSOR FROM ROMNEY LOCK, between Windsor Bridge and Victoria Bridge. The number of motorised boats has increased so that this stretch of the river can be very busy.

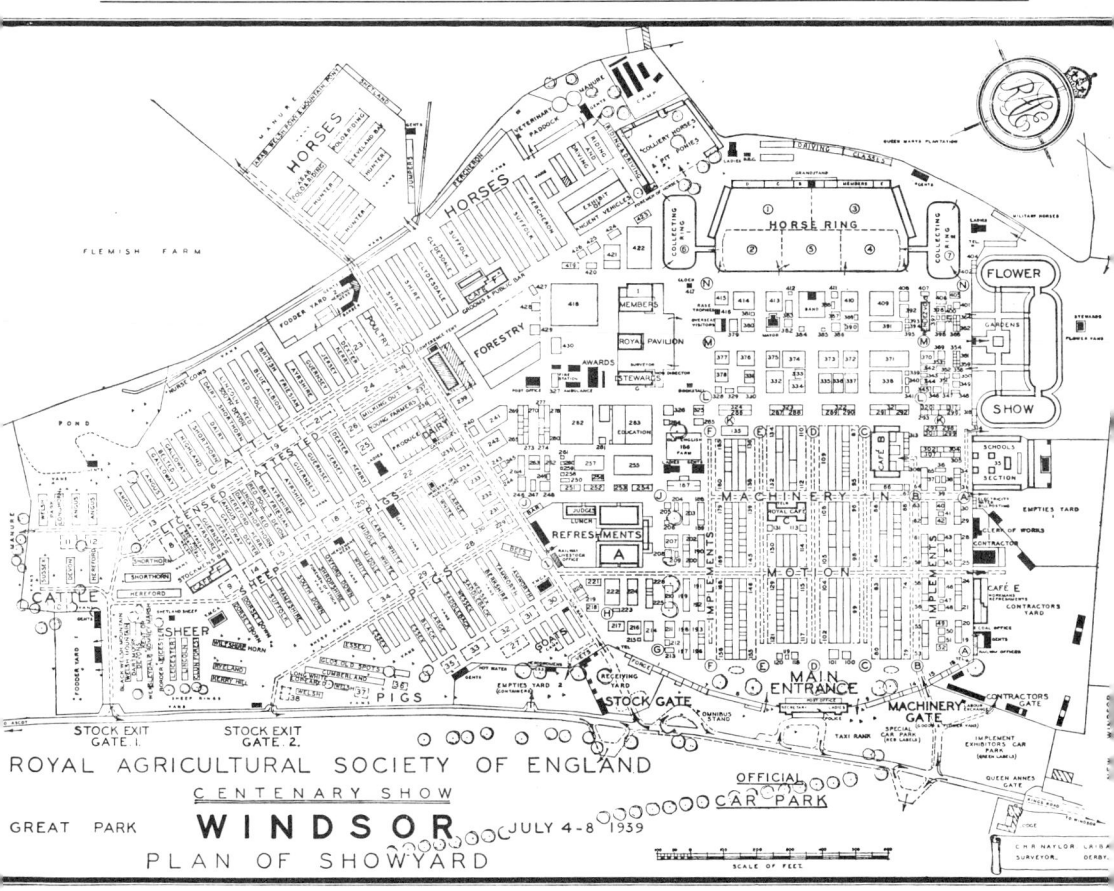

ROYAL AGRICULTURAL SOCIETY OF ENGLAND

CENTENARY SHOW

GREAT PARK **WINDSOR** JULY 4-8 1939

PLAN OF SHOWYARD

THE CENTENARY SHOW OF THE ROYAL AGRICULTURAL SOCIETY in 1939 was the last to be held in Windsor Great Park, as it was not revived here after the war.

THE COVER OF THE CATALOGUE of 196 pages plus advertisements of the show from 4 July to 8 July 1939.

Dorney Church, near Windsor.

AFTER PASSING THROUGH ETON WICK, over the cattle grids and Dorney Common, the delightful village of Dorney is reached. The church of St James has a Norman font and fine monuments, and close by is Dorney Court which is now open to visitors. The first pineapple in Great Britain was grown here.

ACKNOWLEDGEMENTS

Most of the postcards and photographs reproduced in this book are from our own personal collection and grateful acknowledgement is made to the artists and publishers where known for permitting their reproduction. Apologies are tendered for any inadvertant omissions in attribution. I must also acknowledge with thanks the help received from local friends and organisations in its compilation, and especially mention the following:

Mr John Allan, past-Minister, Dedworth Baptist Church • Mr Ronald Bull
Mrs Betty Edwards • Mr Fred Fuzzens • The Revd Ivy Halden, United Reformed Church, Windsor • The Headmaster, Windsor Boys School • Hendon Publishing Mrs Judith Hunter • The Institute of Agricultural History and Museum of English Rural Life, University of Reading • John Lewis Partnership • Mrs Muriel Liddiard Mr John Maxwell • Mrs Parker • The Royal Borough of Windsor and Maidenhead (Royal Borough Collection) • Miss K. Shawcross • Mr E. Shepherd
Mr K. Shepherd • Mr Raymond South • Mr J. Townend, Headmaster, Princess Margaret Royal Free School, Windsor • Mr W. Hall, Editor, *Windsor & Eton Express* • and lastly my husband, David, for his patience and encouragement.